HARAMBE
for the
Holidays

Vibrant Holiday Cooking with Rita Marley

Ordering Information:
Wholesale pricing is available on quantity purchases by dispensaries, retail outlets, bookstores, etc. For details, contact the publisher at the email address below.

Corinne Tobias
corinne@wakeandbakecookbook.com

Printed in the United States of America

Marley, Rita
Wake Up & Live/ RIta Marley
p. 124
ISBN

First Edition
10 9 8 7 6 5 4 3 2 1

Liveacation

To: Bob

Long live the King,
Berhane Selassie,
Light of the Trinity.

This is some of the food that we shared together,
as healing for the mind, soul, and body.
We will be forever loving Jah.

Bless you Bob...

-from Mommy and family

Contents

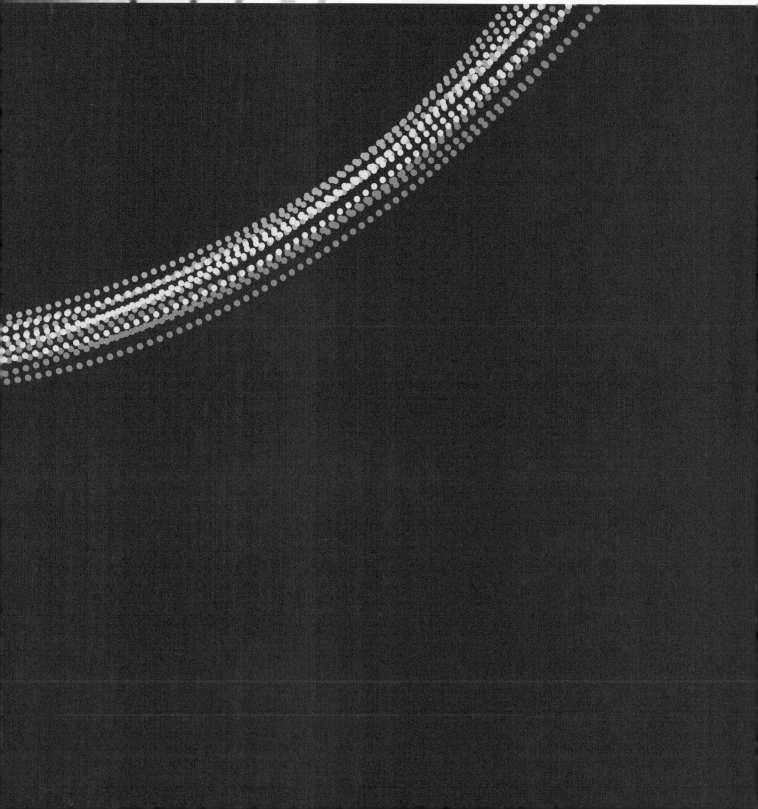

Season's Greetings my Brothers and Sisters!

Blessed holiday to one and all.
Be safe, eat well and stay well.
Remember how green you are!

One Love
One Aim
One Destiny

Rita Marley

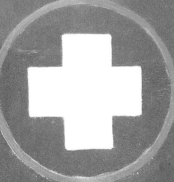 KONKONURU
HEALTH CARE
CENTER

THE
RITA MARLEY
FOUNDATION

THE
BOB MARLEY
TRUST

THE
ANNENBERG
FOUNDATION

THE
PEOPLE OF
KONKONURU

The Rita Marley Foundation

10 % of the proceeds from this book go to support Rita Marley Foundation projects in Ghana, Jamaica and around the world. The foundation provides scholarships, fellowships, emergency grants, health care, education instrument replacement, and community building projects in an effort to disseminate the message of peace, justice, equality, human rights and clean water for health care. The Rita Marley foundation has recently installed several boreholes in Ghana (as seen in the picture) and is currently expanding this clean water project.

More information about programs, volunteering and contributing to the foundation can be found at:

www.ritamarleyfoundation.org

Herb is the Healing of the Nation

Man is like a tree that is planted by the water that brings forth his fruit in due season. His leaves shall not wither and what so ever he do with shall prosper.
-Rita Marley

The hemp plant (scientific name: cannabis, slang: marijuana) is one of the many useful herbs "yielding seed after its kind" created and blessed by God on the third day of creation, "and God saw that it was good." (Genesis 1:12)

God gave herbs for people to use with our free will.

God said, "Behold, I have given you every herb bearing seed which is upon the face of all the earth....To you it will be for meat." ... And God saw everything that he had made, and, behold, it was very good. (Genesis 1:29-31)

The Bible speaks of a special plant. "I will raise up for them a plant of renown, and they shall be no more consumed with hunger in the land, neither bear the shame of the heathen any more." (Ezekiel 34:29)

A healing plant. On either side of the river, was there the tree of life, which bare 12 manner of fruits, and yielding her fruit every month; and the leaves of the tree were for the healing of the nations. (Revelations 22:1-2)

The Herb is a gift from God.

Let the herb be freed and used without penalty or sorrow, then so shall mankind be freed. Now is the time to Wake UP & Live.

When you smoke The Herb,
it reveals you to yourself.

-Bob Marley

Cooking with The Herb

Green OIL

a Wake & Bake recipe

1.

2.

Before you begin: Decarboxylate your marijuana by baking it in the oven at 240° for 1 hour.

Read more about decarboxylation at www.wakeandbakecookbook.com

1. Combine in a crockpot set to warm or low:

**1 Cup Ziggy's Coco'mon Coconut Oil
1 t. Sunflower Lecithin (optional but reccomended)**

Melt. Keep oil around 160° during the entire process for best results.

2. Add

1 Cup Organic Herb (about 1/4 oz.) Decarboxylated

Tools
Crockpot
Cheesecloth
Thermometer
Small Strainer

Stir every half hour or so. After 2-3 hours of heating and steeping, turn off the crock-pot and allow the oil to cool before moving onto the next step.

3. Set up your strainer so it fits snugly in a container. Line with a large piece of cheesecloth.

4. Slowly pour plant matter and oil into the strainer.

5. Using a string or twist tie, gather the cheesecloth around the plant matter and secure.

5.

6.

7.

6. Squeeze any remaining oil out out of the cheesecloth.

7. Pour oil into a pint jar and place in the fridge until cool. Seal with a lid. Store in refrigerator or in a cool, dark place.

Test your dosage before using it in recipes. Always start testing with a safe amount (1/4-1/2 teaspoon) and wait for at least an hour before taking more. Start low and go slow.

Tips

1. Use organically grown Herb for cooking whenever possible.

2. Each "serving" in this book = 1 teaspoon of Green Oil

The strength of the Green Oil will vary depending on the quality of the Herb you use, how it was stored and the method you use for cooking your oil.

Your oil may be effective at anywhere from 1/8th teaspoon-1/2 Tablespoon.

Always test your oil in advance by tasting a small amount on a piece of toast, in a cup of tea or in a smoothie.

3. Decarboxylate and add Sunflower Lecithin when possible to help facilitate absorption and to fully activate THC/CBDs.
(see more at www.wakeandbakecookbook.com)

4. You can always sub regular coconut oil for some or all of the Green Oil to make a recipe less intense or Herb free. You can also use Green Oil in place of Ziggy's Coco'mon Coconut Oil to bring the blessings of the Herb into almost every recipe in this book.

The following are a list of guidelines for using the Herbally blessed recipes this book.

Recipes that use The Herb in this book are only intended for Medical Marijuana Patients and for use in states and nations where the use of The Herb is legal. Outside of those places, the recipes that use Green Oil in this book are intended for entertainment purposes only.

1. Do not operate heavy machinary or drive an automobile after using any of the recipes that use Green Oil.

2. Always label any leftover food that contains Green Oil.

3. Keep Green Oil Recipes Out of Reach of Children, Pets and Unstable Adults.

4. Test your Green Oil before using it in recipes so you know the appropriate dose.

5. Vote to legalize The Herb in your state or nation and support your local movement to

Free The Herb.

Stir
It Up

Sorrel Tea

1. In a small mug, combine:
2 tsp. Dried Sorrel (Hibiscus)
1 Cup boiling Water

2. Cover and
steep for 3
minutes.

3. Add:
1 Tsp. Honey or Agave
(optional)

Sorrel Drink

Directions:

1. Bring water to a boil.
2. Place sorrel, ginger and cloves into boiled water.
3. Boil for 2 minutes, turn heat off.
4. Cover and allow to steep for 12 hours.
5. Strain and sweeten to taste.
6. Add rum or wine if desired.
7. Serve cold, on ice.

Ingredients:

6 cups water
3 cups sorrel, petals
1 ounce ginger root (one inch thick piece)
6 whole pimientos
1 cup granulated sugar

Vegan Eggnog

Ingredients:
1 (12 ounce) package silken soft tofu
1 cup rice milk or soy milk
1/3 cup brown sugar
1 cup apple juice or 1 cup rum
2 teaspoons vanilla
1/8 teaspoon nutmeg
10 -15 ice cubes

Directions:
1. Place the ingredients (except the ice cubes) in blender and blend until smooth.
2. Cover and refrigerate until serving time.
3. To serve, blend the mixture with ice cubes until frothy (you may need to divide liquid in half to fit into blender with ice).
4. Serve in glass sprinkled with nutmeg.

Iced Marley Coffee

a Nice Time recipe

Ingredients:
8 ounces strong brewed Marley Coffee, cold
1/3 cup coconut milk [your choice: lite or full-fat]
3 tablespoons coconut cream
1 teaspoon vanilla extract
2 tablespoons toasted coconut

Directions:
Brew coffee and let cool – this can work with left-over morning coffee, or I suggest making some at night and once it cools, putting it in the fridge overnight. Combine all ingredients except the toasted coconut. Pour over ice, top with toasted coconut, serve!

Cinna'mon Hot Cocoa

1. In a small pot, over med-high heat, combine:

2 Cups Almond Milk
1/4 tsp Vanilla
1/4-1/2 tsp Vietnemese Cinnamon
1 Tblsp Honey or Maple Syrup

2. Whisk in:

2 T Cacao or Cocoa Powder

3. Whisk until smooth. Sprinkle with extra Cinnamon or Pumpkin Pie Spice. Serve warm.

Healing Herb Hot Cocoa

Be aware: Contains The Herb for the Healing of the Nation

1. In a small pot, over med-high heat, combine:

2 Cups Almond Milk
1/2-1 Tblsp Honey
1/4 tsp Vanilla
1/2-1 tsp Green Oil

2. Whisk in:

1 1/2 Tblsp Cacao or Cocoa Powder
1 Tblsp Maca Powder (optional)

3. Whisk until smooth. Serve warm.
Makes 1 Big Mug.

a Wake & Bake recipe

Pumpkin Spice Hot Cocoa

1. In a small pot, over med-high heat, combine:

2 1/2 Cups Almond Milk
1 T Pumpkin Puree
1/4 tsp Vanilla
1/4 tsp Ginger Powder
1 tsp Pumpkin Pie Spice
1 Tblsp Maple or Honey (to taste)

2. Whisk in:

2 T Cacao or Cocoa Powder

3. Whisk until smooth. Sprinkle with **Nutmeg**. Serve warm.

Mocha Mint Hot Cocoa

1. In a small pot, over med-high heat, combine:
2 Cups Almond Milk
1 Cup Marley Coffee
1/8-1/4 tsp Mint Extract
1/4 tsp Vanilla
1/2-1 tsp Green Oil
2. Whisk in:
2 T Cacao or Cocoa Powder
3. Whisk until smooth. Serve warm.
Makes 1 Big Mug.

Don't Worry... About a thing. Because

Every Little Thing

is gonna be allright

(Snacks & Dips)

Party Popcorn

a Wake & Bake recipe

1. In a large pot, over Medium High heat, combine:
2-3 T High Temp Oil (Grapeseed/Sunflower)
3 Unpopped Popcorn Kernels
2. Cover. When the three kernels pop, remove the pot from heat and add:
1/3 Cup Popcorn Kernels
3. Cover and shake the pot to coat the kernels in oil. Count to 30.
4. Place pot back on the heat.
5. Remove when you don't hear much poppin' goin' on anymore.
6. Pour into separate bowls and drizzle with:
1/2-1 t Melted Green Oil (per person)
Salt to Taste

Optional Sweet Step... Melt:
1/2 Cup Vegan Chocolate Chips
2-3 T Coco'mon Coconut Oil
Using a fork, drizzle chocolate over popcorn and top with sprinkles.

Be aware: Contains The Herb for the Healing of the Nation

Artichoke Dip

a Wake & Bake recipe

1. Preheat oven to 375°. In a blender, comibine:

1 ½ Cup Raw Cashews (soaked for 2 hrs)
1 ½ Cup Unsweetened Almond Milk
3-4 Tbsp freshly squeezed lemon juice
2-4 Large Cloves Garlic
2 tsp Nutritional Yeast
1 ½ tsp Sea Salt
1 tsp Ground Mustard
10-12 tsp Green Oil (optional)

2. Empty blender into a large mixing bowl. Stir in:

2 Cans Artichoke Hearts (drained and roughly chopped)
4 cups Thinly Shredded Swiss or Rainbow Chard (can substitute spinach)

3. Pour into a 9 x 13 baking or casserole dish and bake for 25-30 minutes

or

Pour into a 7 x 11 baking or casserole dish and bake for 30-35 minutes, until top is golden and center is warm.

4. If using Green Oil, cool for 15-20 minutes and cut into 10-12 equal portions.

Callaloo Dip

a Nice Time recipe

Ingredients:
2 cups shredded skim mozzarella
1/2 cup fat free sour cream
1/4 cup parmesan cheese
1/4 tsp pepper
16 oz low fat cream cheese
2 1/2 cups cooked, seasoned callaloo (amaranth)
finely minced scotch bonnet pepper, to taste
1 tsp fresh thyme leaves

Directions:
Preheat oven to 350. Combine 1 1/2 cups mozzarella cheese, sour cream, 2 tbs parmesan cheese and the remaining ingredients.
Spread in a baking dish, sprinkle with remaining cheese. Bake for 30 minutes until bubbly. Serve hot with your favorite chips.

Sweet Potato Fries

Ingredients:

2 Pounds Sweet
Potatoes
(about 3 large ones)
3-4 Tbs Coco'mon
Curry Coconut Oil
1-2 Tbsp Sugar
1 Tbsp Salt
1 Tbs Curry Powder
1/2 tsp Cayenne
Pepper

Directions:

1. Preheat oven to 450°F. (For more crispiness, pre-heat your oven to 500°F.)

2. Peel the sweet potatoes and cut off the ends. Cut the potatoes in half lengthwise and then, if they are very long, in half crosswise. Cut each piece into wedges. Alternately, you can slice the peeled sweet potato into disks either with a mandoline or a sharp knife.

3. Put the sweet potatoes into a large bowl and add the cocomon oil. Mix well to combine. Sprinkle with salt, sugar, curry powder and cayenne pepper. Use your hands to mix well, so all pieces are coated with oil and spices.

4. Spread the sweet potatoes out in a single layer on a baking sheet; the oil they are coated with should keep them from sticking to the pan.

5. Bake for a total of 25 to 30 minutes. After the first 15 minutes, remove the baking sheet from the oven and turn over all of the sweet potato pieces. Return to the oven and bake for another 10-15 minutes, or until they are well browned. Let cool for 5 minutes before serving.

Sweet Potato Stacks

a Nice Time recipe

Directions:

1. Preheat oven to 375°. Layer half of sweet potatoes in a lightly greased 12-cup muffin pan. Sprinkle with 1 1/2 tsp. thyme and 1/2 cup cheese. Top with remaining sweet potatoes. (Potatoes will come slightly above the rim of each cup.)

2. Microwave cream, next 3 ingredients, and remaining 1/2 tsp. thyme at HIGH 1 minute. Pour cream mixture into muffin cups (about 1 Tbsp. per cup).

3. Bake at 375°, covered with aluminum foil, 30 minutes. Uncover and sprinkle with remaining 1/2 cup cheese. Bake 5 to 7 minutes or until cheese is melted and slightly golden.

4. Let stand 5 minutes. Run a sharp knife around rim of each cup, and lift potato stacks from cups using a spoon or thin spatula. Transfer to a serving platter. Garnish, if desired.

Ingredients:

1 1/2 pounds small sweet potatoes, peeled and thinly sliced
2 teaspoons chopped fresh thyme, divided
1 cup (4 oz.) freshly shredded mozzarella cheese, divided
2/3 cup heavy cream
1 garlic clove, pressed
1/2 to 3/4 tsp. salt
1/4 teaspoon freshly ground pepper
Garnish: fresh thyme

Cranberry-Kale Salad

1. In a large bowl combine:

4 Cups Kale (finely chopped)
1/4 Cup Olive OIl
Juice of 1/2 Lemon
1/2 Cup Dried Cranberries (Chopped)
1/2 Cup Pecans (Chopped)
1-2 T Nutritional Yeast
or Parmesean
Salt to Taste

2. Toss and serve.

Nut Clusters

1. Preheat oven to 300° and line a baking sheet with parchment paper.
2. In a large mixing bowl, combine:
1/2 Cup Pecan Pieces
1 Cup Walnut Halves
3 Tblsp. Brown Rice Syrup or Honey
3. In a medium mixing bowl, combine:
6 Tblsp. Oats
3 Tblsp. Raw Sugar
1 tsp. Pumpkin Pie Spice
1/4 tsp. Salt
4. Slowly add dry mixture to the sticky nut mixture, stirring often.
5. Spread the mixture onto prepared baking sheet and sprinkle with more Pumpkin Pie Spice or Cinnamon (optional).
6. Bake for 20-25 minutes, rotating the pan once.
7. Cool on the pan for at least 10 minutes before breaking into clusters and transferring to a serving dish or into mason jars for storage.

Gingerbread Snack Bars

a Wake & Bake recipe

1. Preheat oven to 350° and line an 8x8 pan with parchment paper.
2. In a small saucepan over medium heat, melt and combine:

1 Cup Pumpkin Puree
1/3 Cup Organic Molasses
2 Tbls. Green Oil (optional)
1/3 cup Raw Sugar

3. In a food processor, pulse:

1 1/2 Cups Oats

until you have a mix of whole and ground oats.

4. In a large mixing bowl, combine:

Oats
3/4 Cup Flour
1 tsp. Pumpkin Pie Spice or Cinnamon
1/2 tsp. Ginger Powder
1/4 tsp. Salt

5. Add the wet ingredients to the dry, and stir until combined.
6. Scoop the dough into the prepared pan, cover with a second peice of parchment paper, and press until mixture is evenly spread out.
7. Bake for 20-25 Minutes, until firm.
Cool for 30 minutes before slicing into 8 bars.
8. In a medium mixing bowl, combine maple icing ingredients:

2 T Cashew Butter
1 T Maple Syrup
2 tsp. Green Oil (optional)
1/4 tsp. Pumpkin Spice

8. Scoop Maple Icing into a sandwich baggie and snip off the bottom corner. Cut into 8 equal bars. Evenly distribute Maple Icing on each bar.
Serves 8

Holiday Spice Pan Granola

a Wake & Bake recipe

Be aware: Contains The Herb for the Healing of the Nation

1. In a large pan over medium heat, combine:
1/4 Cup Coco'mon Coconut Oil
2 Tbsp. Green Oil (optional)
1/2 Cup Maple Syrup
2. Once melted, stir in:
2 1/2 Cups Oats
3. Cook, stirring frequently until oats begin to turn golden, but are still sticky. Add:
1/2 Cup Chopped and Whole Almonds
1 tsp. Pumpkin Pie Spice
1/2 tsp. Cinnamon
4. When oats and nuts turn golden, turn down the heat and stir in:
1/4 Cup Cranberries (Chopped)
or Raisins or Currants

Serves 6

MMMmango Pan Granola

1. In a large pan over medium heat, combine:
1/4 Cup +2 Tbsp. Coco'mon Coconut Oil
1/2 Cup Honey or Agave
2. Once melted, stir in:
2 1/2 Cups Oats
3. Cook, stirring frequently until oats begin to turn golden, but are still sticky. Add:
1/2 Cup Sunflower Seeds
1/4 tsp. Nutmeg
1/2 tsp. Cinnamon
4. When oats and nuts turn golden, turn down the heat and stir in:
1/4 Cup Dried Mango (Chopped)

Berry Merry Pan Granola

a Wake & Bake recipe

Be aware: Contains The Herb for the Healing of the Nation

1. In a large pan over medium heat, combine:
1/4 Cup Coco'mon Coconut Oil
2 Tbsp. Green Oil (optional)
1/2 Cup Maple Syrup
2. Once melted, stir in:
2 1/2 Cups Oats
3. Cook, stirring frequently until oats begin to turn golden, but are still sticky. Add:
1/2 Cup Chopped Pecans
1 tsp. Pumpkin Pie Spice
1/2 tsp. Cinnamon
4. When oats and nuts turn golden, turn down the heat and stir in:
1/4 Cup Dried Blueberries
or Blackberries or Raspberries

Serves 6

Let's

Get Together

and feel all right

Callaloo Tart

Ingredients:

For the crust:
2 cups flour
8 tablespoons chilled coco'mon coconut oil
¼ tsp. kosher salt
1 tablespoon milk
1 egg, lightly beaten

For the filling:
2 tablespoons coco'mon coconut oil
3 cloves garlic, minced
1 large yellow onion, minced
½ red bell pepper, stemmed, seeded, and minced
½ Scotch bonnet seeded, and minced
1 large bunch callaloo (amaranth), well-rinsed, ends trimmed, chopped
1/4 cup veggie broth
8 oz. sharp cheddar cheese, grated
½ cup whole milk
6 eggs, salt and freshly ground black pepper, to taste

Directions:

Make the crust:
1. Combine flour, coconut oil, and salt in a food processor. Pulse until pea-size crumbles form. Add milk and egg, and pulse until dough forms. Shape dough into a disk, and wrap in plastic wrap; chill for 1 hour.

2. Roll out the dough to about 1/4 thick and place in tart pan. Chill until ready to use.

Make the filling:
1. Preheat oven to 425 degrees.
Heat coconut oil in large saucepan over medium-high heat. Add garlic, onion, pepper, and scotch bonnet, and cook, stirring until softened, about 10 minutes.

2. Add the callaloo and veggie broth, and cook until the callaloo is wilted and the liquid has largely evaporated, about 2-3 minutes.

3. Transfer to a bowl then stir in 6 oz. cheddar, milk, and eggs. Season with salt and pepper. Pour into prepared crust and top with remaining cheddar. Bake until golden brown and set, about 30 minutes.

Kale Bake

Ingredients:

1 Tbsp coco'mon coconut oil
1 bunch kale, about 7 oz, center ribs removed, (leaves thinly sliced)
Salt and freshly ground black pepper
6 ounces mushrooms of choice, finely chopped
1 small bunch scallion, thinly sliced
1/2 a scotch bonnet pepper, seeded and minced
1-2 cloves fresh minced garlic
1 tsp fresh thyme leaves
1/2 loaf bread, about 12 thin slices,
(try jamaican hardough bread or ciabatta bread)
3 large eggs
1 1/2 cups milk

Directions:

1. Grease an 8-inch square baking dish with a little coconut oil and set aside.

2. Heat the cocomon coconut oil in a large skillet on medium heat. Add the thinly sliced kale and cook until just wilted, about 2 to 3 minutes.

3. Add the scallion, mushrooms, garlic, scotch bonnet and thyme, add salt and pepper to taste. Increase the heat to medium high and cook, stirring frequently, until the mushrooms have released their moisture and the onions are translucent, 3 to 5 minutes. Remove from heat and let cool for 5 minutes.

4. In a medium bowl, whisk together the milk and eggs.

5. Line the bottom of the casserole pan with one third of the thinly sliced bread. Spread one half of the kale mushroom scallion mixture over the bread. Sprinkle one third of the cheddar cheese over the top. Lay down the second third of the bread slices. Top again with the remaining kale mixture, and then with a third of the cheese. Lay the remaining slices of bread over the top.

6. Pour the milk egg mixture over the bread, pressing down with a spatula so that the milk is absorbed by the casserole layers. Sprinkle the top with the remaining cheddar cheese. (you can chill this overnight for making ahead, or continue.)

7. Let the casserole sit for about 15 minutes to further absorb the milk while you preheat the oven to 350°F. Cover with foil. Bake covered for 30 minutes, then remove the foil and bake an additional 25 to 30 minutes, until the cheese is golden and bubbly. Let the casserole sit for a few minutes before serving.

Jah Blessed Mashed Potatoes

Be aware: Contains The Herb for the Healing of the Nation

a Wake & Bake recipe

1. Preheat oven to 425°
2. Cut the top off of:
   1 Head Garlic
3. Drizzle garlic with Olive Oil and cover with tinfoil. Bake until fragrant and tender (about 30-40 minutes).
4. In a large stockpot, combine:
   2 Pounds of Potatoes
   Cold Water (enough to cover potatoes)
   Salt
5. Bring to a boil and cook until fork tender.
6. Once potatoes are tender and garlic is roasted, remove garlic cloves and smash with a wooden spoon. Drain the potatoes and mash until smooth.
7. In a large mixing bowl, combine:
   Mashed Potatoes
   Smashed Garlic
   1 T Dried Parsley Flakes
   1/2-1 tsp Onion Powder (optional)
   2 T Green Oil
   3 T Coco'mon Coconut Oil
   1/2-3/4 Cup Almond milk *unsweetened)
8. Mash all ingredients until smooth. Serve warm.

Serves: 6 depending on the strength of your oil. Test your doseage before using in recipes. This recipe contains 6 tsp servings of Green Oil.

Pumpkin Chili

Ingredients:

2 cups dried kidney beans, soaked overnight in 5 cups of water
3 cloves garlic, smashed
1 inch piece ginger, peeled and smashed
1 cup coconut milk
1 small onion, chopped
1 small bell pepper, chopped
3 cloves garlic, minced
1 minced scotch bonnet pepper
1 tbs. Ziggy Marley Cocomon coconut oil
3 cups diced pumpkin
1 package veggie crumbles
1 28 oz. can crushed tomatoes
2 cups brewed Marley Coffee
2 tsp chili powder
2 tsp oregano
Salt and pepper to taste

Directions:

1. In a large pot, bring soaked beans in water, 3 cloves smashed garlic, ginger and coconut milk to a boil.

2. Reduce heat to medium low and simmer until beans are soft.

3. In a separate pan, saute onion, bell pepper, minced garlic and scotch bonnet pepper in coconut oil until translucent.

4. Add all remaining ingredients to the pot of beans, as well as the onions and peppers from the separate pan.

5. Simmer chili over low heat for at least 45 minutes, stirring occasionally. Then serve.

a Nice Time recipe

Ethiopian Genna Dinner

In the Marley home, we celebrate our time of giving by the Ethiopian calendar on January 7th…otherwise known as Genna. It is one of my favorite times of year, as the entire family, well almost the entire family, comes over.

We eat, laugh, love, and of course give thanks. Celebrate Genna with us this year. Prepare this meal on January 7th and share it with your family.

One Love & Happy Genna,
Cedella Marley

Ethiopian Tomato Salad

Directions:

1. Combine jalapeno, onions, lemon juice, and black pepper in a bowl.

2. Stir in tomatoes.

3. Add salt to taste.

4. Chill before serving.

Ingredients:

1 jalapeno pepper, seeded and minced
1/4 cup chopped red onions
1 1/2 tablespoons lemon juice
1/4 teaspoon black pepper
3 ripe tomatoes, chopped
salt, to taste

Tilkil Gomen
(potato cabbage)

Directions:

1. In a large pot, cook the onions, stirring occasionally, on medium/medium-high heat until they start to soften and turn translucent, about 5-7 minutes.

2 Add the oil (as much as your arteries can take!) and cook until the oil gets hot. Add the turmeric, stir to ensure that it is evenly distributed, and cook for another few minutes (and please be sure to take a second to enjoy the aroma). Add the scallions and cook for another minute or two.

3. Add the water and bring to a boil on medium-high heat. Once the water is boiling, add the potatoes, stir, and cover. Since the potatoes take longer to cook than the other vegetables, let them cook for at least 5-10 minutes. Then add the carrots, cover again and allow them to cook for several minutes, and add the cabbage.

4. Add the salt and continue cooking until the cabbage starts to shrink and soften. When the potatoes are almost finished cooking, add the basil, ginger, garlic, and jalapeno peppers and cook until the vegetables are tender.

Ingredients:

2-3 onions, chopped
1/3-1/2+ cup sunflower oil
1-2 tbsp. turmeric
3/4 cup water
4-5 Yukon gold potatoes, cut in half lengthwise then sliced into 1/4-1/2 inch pieces
3-4 carrots, chopped into stick-shaped pieces
1 head green cabbage, chopped
6 scallions (white parts with some of the green), chopped
1 1/2 tbsp. dried basil
finely chopped garlic
finely chopped ginger
salt (to taste)
2 jalapeno peppers, seeds removed and sliced into thin strips

Misir Wot
(red lentils)

Ingredients:

2 Onions chopped
2 cloves Garlic crushed
2 t Ginger root, peeled, minced
¼ c Oil, butter or niter kibbeh
1 t Turmeric
2 T Paprika
½ to 2 t Cayenne Pepper
1 lb Red Lentils
4 c Water or Stock
Salt & Pepper to taste

Directions:

1. Puree onion, garlic, and ginger in a food processor or blender.

2 Heat oil, butter or niter kibbeh in a large, heavy-bottomed saucepan. Add turmeric, paprika and cayenne pepper and stir rapidly to color oil and cook spices through, about 30 seconds. Add onion puree and sauté on medium heat until excess moisture evaporates and onion loses its raw aroma, about 5-10 minutes. Do not burn.

3. Add lentils and water. Bring to a boil and simmer till lentils are cooked through and fall apart, about 30-40 minutes. Add water if necessary to keep from drying out. Stir in salt and pepper to taste and serve.

Ethiopian Tempeh Tibs

Ingredients:

2 8 oz. Packages Tempeh
4 tablespoons Sunflower Oi
2 tablespoon berbere*
Salt
1 large tomato, diced
1 medium onion, diced

Directions:

1. In a large bowl add the veggie chunks or tempeh and 2 tablespoons of olive oil. Season with the berbere and salt, to taste. Let the chunks marinate with spices for about 30 minutes.

2. Put remaining 2 tablespoons of olive oil in a medium saucepan and put over medium heat. Add the tomatoes and onions and stir for 5 minutes. Add the marinated veggie chunks or tempeh and cook for another 10 minutes, stirring consistently.

3. Once the liquid in the pan begins to boil continue cooking for another 5 minutes. Remove the pan from heat and stir in the jalapenos.

4. Serve with Injera

*Can be found at specialty Indian and Middle Eastern markets or you can blend your own

Overnight Injera
(Ethiopian Sourdough Crepe)

Ingredients:
1 lb Teff Flour
3 cups of luke warm water
1 teaspoon of yeast *

Directions:

1. Mix by hand, 1lb of Teff with 3 cups of water along with 1 teaspoon of yeast.

2. Set aside overnight (24 hrs) outside. For fermentation to take place.

3. Preheat pan, and leave on low heat

4. Pour in a circular motion, same as a pancake. Only heated on one side, takes about 2 minutes.

5. Take injera out carefully (hot) and set aside on a plate to cool down before eating.

If this is your first batch of injera, use the teaspoon of yeast; but if you plan to make injera regularly… then save about 3 soup spoons of the mix for your next injera. This will act as a self rising yeast on your next batch of injera; save it in your fridge it will stay for over a month. This is the same process of saving some of your current dough for your next batch of sour dough cakes or cookies.

In this life, In this life, in this oh

Sweet Life

we're comin' in from the cold

and we never grow old...

Almond Lace Cookies

Directions:

1. Preheat the oven to 275° and line 2 baking sheets with parchment paper.

2. Chop the sliced almonds into small pieces and add them to a bowl with the Flour, Orange Zest, Salt and Sugar.

3. In a small saucepan, over medium high heat, combine Coco'mon Coconut Oil, Brown Rice Syrup, and Coconut Milk. Stir just until the mixture comes to a low boil. Remove from heat and add Vanilla.

3. Add the dry ingredients to the soucepan and mix until combined. Allow to cool for 10 minutes, or until the mixture is cool enough to handle with your fingers.

4. Using a Tablespoon, skoop mixture onto the prepared baking sheets, leaving about 3-4 inches of space in between the cookies.

5. Bake 15-17 minutes, rotating the pan once during baking. Cool on sheet for at least 5 minutes before moving them onto a cooling rack.

6. In a double boiler, melt chocolate chips. Using a fork, drizzle chocolate over cookies and sprinkle with powdered sugar.

Ingredients:

2 cups sliced almonds
3 tbsp gluten-free all-purpose flour (or other flour)
1 tbsp powdered orange zest
1/4 tsp salt
1/2 cup sugar
1/4 cup Coco'mon coconut oil
2 tbsp brown rice syrup
2 tbsp full-fat canned coconut milk
1 tsp vanilla
1/4-1/3 cup dark chocolate chips
1/2 tsp coconut oil
powdered sugar (optional)

a Wake & Bake recipe
Gingerbread

Ingredients:

1 flax egg (1 Tbsp flax + 3 Tbsp water)
or 1 chicken egg
1/2 cup brown sugar
1/4 cup almond butter
3 Tbsp molasses
1/4 cup Green Oil (room temperature)
3/4 tsp Ginger
1/2 tsp Cinnamon
1/4 tsp nutmeg
1/4 tsp salt
1/2 tsp baking soda
1 1/4 - 1 3/4 cups flour

Directions:

1. In a large mixing bowl, cominbe flax and water. Let your flax egg chill for about 5 minutes.
2. Add Brown Sugar, Almond Butter, Molasses, Green Oil, Ginger, Cinnamon, Nutmeg, Salt and Baking Soda. Beat on low.
3. Add flour 1/2 cup at a time and mix until the dough holds together, but is not sticky or dry.
3. Chill for a few hours or overnight.
4. Preheat oven to 375°
5. Roll dough into 1 Tablespoon sized balls and freeze for 10 minutes.
6. Bake about 10-12 minutes, until they are just slightly browned at the edges. No worries. They'll firm up as they cool.

Serves: 12 depending on the strength of your oil. Test your dosage before using in recipes. This recipe contains 12 tsp servings.

Stuffed Apples

a Nice Time recipe

Directions:

1. Preheat the oven to 375°. In a medium bowl, mix the almonds with the ginger snap crumbs, currants or raisins, brown sugar, cinnamon and lemon zest. Add the coconut oil and mix with your fingers until the filling resembles coarse meal.

2. Using a sharp knife, cut a 1/4-inch-thick slice from the top and bottom of each apple. Working from the stem end and using a melon baller, apple corer or sharp knife, remove the interior core and seeds to within 1/2 inch of the bottom. Using a paring or channeling knife, score the apple skin lengthwise at 1 1/2-inch intervals. Arrange the apples so they don't touch in an 8-inch square baking dish and spoon the filling into them, mounding any remaining filling on top. Pour the apple juice and rum around the apples.

3. Bake the apples for 20 minutes. Cover loosely with foil and bake for 45 to 50 minutes longer, or until the apples are very soft. Transfer the apples to plates with a spatula. Spoon the pan juices on top and serve.

Ingredients:

3 tablespoons slivered blanched almonds, lightly toasted

2-3 ounces ginger snap cookies, crushed

1/3 cup dried currants or raisins

2 tablespoons dark brown sugar

1/2 teaspoon cinnamon

Finely grated zest of 1 lemon

2 tablespoons common coconut oil

4 Fuji apples (about 7 ounces each)

1 cup apple juice

2 tablespoons Spice Root Rum

Apple Crisp

1. Grease an 8x8 pan with coconut oil. Oven = 350°
2. In a large mixing bowl, combine:
   6 Apples (sliced ¼ inch thick)
   2-3 T Sugar
   ¾ t Cinnamon
   ¼ t Salt
3. Pour Coated Apples into prepped pan.
4. In the bowl used for apples, combine:
   ½ Cup Brown Sugar
   ½ Cup Rolled Oats
   1/3 Cup Flour
   ¼ Cup Green Oil*
   (cold & cut into small chunks)
5. Pour Oat Mixuture over apples.
6. Bake 45 minutes to 1 hr, until topping is crispy and apples are soft. Serve warm.

Serves: 12 depending on the strength of your oil. Test your dosage before using in recipes. This recipe contains 12 tsp servings of Green Oil.

Cornmeal Pudding

Preheat oven to 375°

1. In a large mixing bowl, combine:
5 Cups Coconut Milk (2 Cans)
1/2 Cup Brown Sugar

2. **In a separate bowl, combine:**
2 Cups Cornmeal
1/2 Cup Taosted Coconut
1/2 Cup Flour
1/2 Cup Brown Sugar
1 t Cinnamon
1 t Nutmeg
1 t Allspice

3. Slowly mix dry ingredients into wet ingredients.

4. Stir in:
1 Cup Raisins

Bake for 50-60 Minutes until the top is golden and a knife inserted into the center comes out mostly clean.

Jamaican Christmas Cake

This is a traditional Jamaican cake made for the holidays. It can be baked like a regular cake in the oven, but the traditional way is to steam it in boiling water.

Ingredients:

½ pound butter
1 cup sugar
2 tablespoons burnt sugar or browning
1 ½ cups all purpose flour
1 teaspoon baking powder
1/2 teaspoon salt
1 teaspoon ground cinnamon
1/4 teaspoon ground nutmeg
1/4 teaspoon ground allspice
Zest of 1 Lemon
4 eggs
1 ¼ cups red wine or brandy
16 ounces raisins
1/2 candied cherries, pitted and chopped
1 cup prunes, chopped
¼ cup Rum

Directions:

1. Grate the peel of a lemon to create zest. Pitt and coarsely chop the cherries and prunes. Place the zest, cherries, raisins, and prunes in a container with a tight lid, cover with wine or brandy and soak for at least a week, longer if possible. This mixture can soak for months if you plan ahead!

Sift or mix together in a large bowl the flour, baking powder, salt, cinnamon, nutmeg, and allspice.

2. Cream butter, sugar, and burnt sugar in a bowl. Mix until smooth. Add the egg mixture to the butter mixture and mix thoroughly. Then stir in the soaked fruit to the mixture.

3. Slowly fold in the dry ingredients to the egg, fruit, butter mixture and blend completely.

4. Preheat the oven to 350. Line a cake tin with parchment paper on the bottom and sides. Pour the cake batter into the cake pan. Tightly wrap the entire pan with aluminum foil, so it is sealed as well as possible. Place sealed cake in a deep casserole dish. Fill casserole dish with enough boiling water to cover the sides of the cake, but not the top. Put the whole thing in the oven and bake for 4 hours, occasionally checking to add more water as needed.

5. Remove cake from oven, unwrap when its cool enough and pour the rum over the top of cake.

Pumpkin Marley Rum Cake

Directions:

1. Preheat oven to 325°. Grease a 12-cup bundt pan; sprinkle pecans evenly over the bottom of the pan; set aside.
2. In a large mixing bowl, add flour, all the spices, baking soda, and salt; stir to combine.
3. In another large mixing bowl, add 1 cup butter, 1 cup sugar, and brown sugar; beat with an electric mixer until light and fluffy.
   - Add eggs; beat well to combine.
   - Add pumpkin and vanilla; beat well to combine.
4. Add flour mixture to batter one-third at a time, mixing well after each addition.
5. Pour batter into tube pan.
6, Bake for 60-70 minutes or until pick comes out clean. Let cool 10 minutes.
7. To make glaze: melt the remainder of the butter in a saucepan.
8. Add in the remaining sugar and water; stir and bring to a boil (add more water sparingly if not the consistency you want).
9. Remove pan from heat; add in rum; stir to combine.
10. Poke holes in cake with a toothpick.
11. Pour half the rum mixture over the cake.
12. Let stand 5 minutes.
13. Pour the rest of the rum mixture over the cake.
14. Cool.

Ingredients:

3/4 cup chopped pecans
3 cups all-purpose flour
2 tsp ground cinnamon
1 tsp ground ginger
1/2 tsp fresh ground nutmeg
1/2 tsp ground allspice
2 teaspoons baking soda
1 teaspoon salt
1 1/4 cups butter, softened, divided
1 1/2 cups sugar, divided
1 cup packed brown sugar
4 large eggs
1 (15 ounce) can pumpkin
1 teaspoon vanilla extract
2 tablespoons water

Raw Cranberry Citrus Cake

Crust

1. In a food processor, process until malleable:
1 1/2 Cup Figs
3/4 Cup Sunflower Seeds
1/4 t Salt
2. Press into a 9" cake pan and refrigerate for 30 minutes.

Filling

1. In a food processor or high speed blender, combine the following until smooth (blender is best for this step):
3/4 Cup Coconut Flour
1.5 Cups Soaked Cashews
2 Bananas
2 Oranges, Zest and Fruit
1 Cup Cocomon Coconut Oil (melted)
1/3 t Turmeric
1/2 t Vanilla
2. Pour over crust and refrigerate overnight or freeze for 4 hrs.

Vanilla Frosting

1. In a high speed blender, combine until smooth:
3/4 Cup Cashews (soaked for 3-5 hrs)
6 T Coconut Butter
3 t + Lemon Jiuice
1/3 t Vanilla
1/3 t Powdered Ginger
1 1/2 t Honey or Agave
2. Spread onto cake and top with:
Dried Cranberries (Chopped)

Coco' mon Cheesecake

Directions:

1. Stir together crushed graham crackers and Cocomon coconut oil; press mixture into bottom and up sides of a 9-inch springform pan coated with cooking spray.

2. Bake at 350° for 10 minutes. Cool on a wire rack. Reduce oven temperature to 325°.

3. Beat cream cheese and sugar and molasses at medium speed with an electric mixer until blended. Add coffee, vanilla, and ground coffee, beating at low speed until well blended. Add eggs, 1 at a time until everything is blended smooth.

4. Remove and reserve 1 cup cream cheese mixture. Pour remaining batter into prepared crust.

5. Microwave grated cocoa with 1-2 Tbs milk in a small, microwave-safe bowl, 30 sec to a minute, until melted. Stir reserved 1 cup cream cheese mixture into melted chocolate, blending well. Spoon mixture in lines on top of batter in pan; gently swirl with a knife.

6. Bake at 325° for 1 hour or until almost set. Turn oven off. Let cheesecake stand in oven, with door closed, 30 minutes. Remove cheesecake from oven, and gently run a knife around outer edge of cheesecake to loosen from sides of pan. (Do not remove sides of pan.) Cool 1 hour on a wire rack. Cover and chill at least 4 hours.

Ingredients:

2 cups crushed graham crackers (about 18 crackers)
1/3 cup Cocomon coconut oil
Vegetable cooking spray
4 (8-oz.) packages reduced-fat cream cheese, softened
3/4 cup sugar
1/4 cup molasses
1/3 cup extra strong brewed Marley coffee, cooled
1 teaspoon vanilla extract
1 Tbs finely ground Marley coffee
4 large eggs
1 ball Jamaican chocolate, finely grated
2 Tbs milk

Pumpkin Spice Ice Cream

Be aware: Contains The Herb for the Healing of the Nation

1. Line an 8X8 inch pan with parchment paper.
2. Shake up:
   2 Cans of Full Fat Coconut Milk (not lite)
3. Open and pour the cans of coconut milk into the parchment lined pan.
4. Freeze for a few hours or overnight.
5. Using a knife, cut ¼ chunk of the frozen coconut milk out of the pan. If it got super frozen, leave it out to thaw for a half hour to an hour.
6. In a food processor, combine:
   Frozen Coconut Milk Chunk
   1/2 t vanilla
   1-2 T Maple Syrup
   Pinch or Two of Cinnamon (optional)
   Pinch of Salt
   1-2 t Cannabis Infused Oil (melted)*
6.a. Stir in optional chunky ingredients (chunks of chocolate/cookies/hot fudge swirl/etc.)
7. Once Smooth, pour into a small glass container. Immediately put in the freezer.
8. Every 10 minutes, stir until it gets firm enough to scoop out (about 30 minutes).

Serves: 1-2 depending on the strength of your oil. Test your dosage before using in recipes. This recipe contains 1 tsp serving of Green Oil.

a Wake & Bake recipe

Marley Mint Ice Cream

1. Line an 8X8 inch pan with parchment paper.
2. Shake up:
   2 Cans of Full Fat Coconut Milk (not lite)
3. Open and pour the cans of coconut milk into the parchment lined pan.
4. Freeze for a few hours or overnight.
5. Using a knife, cut ¼ chunk of the frozen coconut milk out of the pan. If it got super frozen, leave it out to thaw for a half hour to an hour.
6. In a food processor, combine:
   Frozen Coconut Milk Chunk
   1/4 t vanilla
   1-2 T Honey
   Pinch of Salt
   1/2 T Cacao or Cocoa Powder
   1/8 t Organic Mint Extract

6.a. Stir in optional chunky ingredients (chunks of chocolate/cookies/hot fudge swirl/etc.)
7. Once Smooth, pour into a small glass container. Immediately put in the freezer.
8. Every 10 minutes, stir until it gets firm enough to scoop out (about 30 minutes). Repeat the process to make more than 1-2 servings.

Gingerbread Ice Cream

1. Line an 8X8 inch pan with parchment paper.
2. Shake up:
   2 Cans of Full Fat Coconut Milk (not lite)
3. Open and pour the cans of coconut milk into the parchment lined pan.
4. Freeze for a few hours or overnight.
5. Using a knife, cut ¼ chunk of the frozen coconut milk out of the pan. If it got super frozen, leave it out to thaw for a half hour to an hour.
6. In a food processor, combine:
   Frozen Coconut Milk Chunk
   1/2 t vanilla
   1-2 T Maple Syrup
   Pinch or Two of Cinnamon
   Pinch of Salt
   1/2 tsp Ginger
   1/2 tsp Molasses
   1/4 tsp Nutmeg
6.a. Stir in:
   1-2 Gingerbread Cookies (crumbled)
7. Once Smooth, pour into a small glass container. Immediately put in the freezer.
8. Every 10 minutes, stir until it gets firm enough to scoop out (about 30 minutes).

Crispy Treats

a Wake & Bake recipe

1. Grease an 8x8 pan or line it with parchment paper.
2. In a saucepan over low-med heat, melt:
   - **¼ Cup Nut Butter**
   - **½ Cup Brown Rice Syrup (+1 T Agave or Honey... optional)**
   - **2 T Green Oil**
   - **2 T Coco'mon Coconut Oil**
   - **1 T Vanilla**
3. Pour mixture into a large bowl and slowly incorporate:
   - **3 ½ Cups Rice Crispies**
4. Pour the mixture into the pan and press even with a big wooden spoon or spatula.
5. Refrigerate for 30 minutes-1hr. Keep refrigerated until ready to serve.

Serves: 6 depending on the strength of your oil. Test your dosage before using in recipes. This recipe contains 6 tsp servings of Green Oil.

Be aware: Contains The Herb for the Healing of the Nation

Gingerbread Truffles

1. In a Food Processor, chop:
   2 Cups of Walnuts or Pecans
2. Once roughly chopped, add:
   6-8 Dates
   2 T Maple Syrup
   1 t Cinnamon
   1 t Ginger Powder
   Dash of Nutmeg
   Pinch of Salt
3. Process until the ingredients are fully combined and dough-y.
4. Roll "dough" into truffles and roll the truffles in:
   Shredded Coconut (toasted if possible)
until covered.
5. Refrigerate before serving.

Coconut Cut Cake

Ingredients:
1 Cup reshly chopped or grated coconut.
2 Inches Fresh Ginger
7 tsp Cane sugar

Directions:
Boil 2 cups of water and 7 tsps of cane sugar.
After blended add coconut and cook for
2 hours until mixture is tight.

Spoon desired size drop onto a
parchment paper lined baking sheet.
Cool to harden.

Sprinkle with Ziggy Marley Hemp Rules hemp seeds
(toasted or un toasted).

Nana Rita's Special

Harambe

Sorbet

Harambe means "Working Together in Unity"

This healthy layered sorbet takes some time creating and is a real labor of love.
It represent the true meaning of "Harambe".

Green

1 Large Avocado
1 1/2 cup of water
Juice of 1/2 lemon
1 lime
2 oranges
2 Tsp agave or honey

Gold

1 Lb. chopped pineapple
3/4 cup Coconut milk creamer or cream of your choice
2 Tsp Maple flavored agave

Red

4 small to medium chopped raw beets
2 inches peeled chopped or grated ginger
1/3 cup coconut milk creamer
1 1/2 cup of water
2 Tbls agave or honey

Blend each separately in blender. Freeze each separately stirring occasionally until ice cream reaches the desired consistency

We love the texture of the ground fibers as opposed to juicing.

One Love
One Aim
One Destiny

Contributors

Wake Up & Live Photos
Contributed by: Serita Mazza Antoinette Stewart

The Serita Mazza Antoinette Stewart photographs are from Mrs. Marley's washbelly (her last child), who has a great future ahead of her. She has traveled the world as Mrs. Marley's personal photographer.

Contributors

Wake & Bake
Recipes and Photos,
Book Layout & Design

Contributed by: Corinne Tobias
More info and recipes @
www.wakeandbakecookbook.com

Ziggy Marley Organics

Throughout this book, you'll see Ziggy Marley's line of Organic Coconut Oils and Hemp Seeds in many of the recipes. We love them! And not just because they're from Ziggy.

Ziggy Marley's Hemp Rules™ hempseeds are USDA certified organic and provide an excellent source of protein, containing more of the nine essential amino acids than soy or eggs. Hemp Rules hempseeds also provide Omega fatty acids with the recommended 3:1 Omega-6 to Omega-3 ratio.

Ziggy Marley's Coco'Mon™ coconut oils are made from fresh organic coconut kernels and are cold-pressed, unrefined, non-deodorized, gluten free and kosher. They are an excellent source of medium chain-triglycerides (MCTs), such as lauric acid (C-12) and caprylic acid (C-8).

Find out more at: www.ziggymarleyorganics.com

Marley Coffee

The delicious and rich Marley Coffee is used in many of the recipes in this book (even in an incredible pumpkin chili!).

Rohan Marley is the founder of Marley Coffee. Rohan is a passionate entrepreneur and visionary, like his father, combining his creativity and business acumen to create a self-sustainable and certified organic coffee farm which aims to help preserve Earth's natural balance.

Marley Coffee has seen rapid growth in the gourmet marketplace, thanks to the rich, bold flavors of their coffee beans, and to Rohan's unwavering support of sustainable, organic, and Fair Trade farming practices.

Stir it up!

Find out more at: www.marleycoffee.com

Cedella Marley
Co-Author

Cedella Marley is
the fashion designer and
cook behind
www.anicetime.com

She is passionate about
creating delicious and
healthy recipes for
everyone!

From Mama's Hands to You

Mama's hand are like no other whatever
she touches taste like butter. " Hello there Sweetie "
she calls when we enter.
Mama's hands hold Legends of old ,
her wisdom is wiser than silver or gold.
Mama's secrets are yours now too
as she give a big welcome
" Hello Sweetie" to you !

Rita Marley

Rita Marley is a world-renown musician who loves cooking family meals that heal the body, mind and soul.

As the founder of the Rita Marley Foundation, Mrs. Marley is passionate about helping communities in Jamaica , Ghana and around the world to promote the ideals of peace, justice, human rights and accessibility to clean water for all.

"Don't jump in the water if you can't swim."

-Nana Rita

CPSIA information can be obtained at www.ICGtesting.com
Printed in the USA
BVOW11s2349151214

379531BV00019B/454/P